THEN AND NOW

2023

BY

MADELINE SHARPLES

ISBN: 978-81-19228-39-3

First Edition: 2023
Rs. 200/-

Cyberwit.net
HIG 45 Kaushambi Kunj, Kalindipuram
Allahabad - 211011 (U.P.) India
http://www.cyberwit.net
Tel: +(91) 9415091004
E-mail: info@cyberwit.net

Printed at Replika Press.

Contents

THEN

1. The Last Year

Finding Things for Bob

My husband is always losing things:
his glasses, his keys, his checkbook.
Yesterday it was his bottle
of cough medicine.
He clearly remembered
he had bought a big bottle
but as usual, asked me if I had seen it.
I suggested two places:
the top shelf in the kitchen cabinet
where we store other medical stuff
or the brown woven tray
next to his bathroom sink.
It wasn't on the shelf – I could attest to that,
and according to him he couldn't find it
on the woven tray
But somehow I could.
As I was preparing for bed last night
I looked over there,
and saw it in the back row.
I got it out, complete with its little plastic dosage cup,
and left it for him to find when he woke this morning.
Sure enough he did and asked me where I found it.
Well duh? Right where you didn't see it, my love.
But my finding it
didn't even rate a kiss, a hug,
or even a thank you.

Bob Cooked!

A surprise! Bob actually cooked.
He made himself scrambled eggs
with cheese and salsa this very morning.
I didn't want eggs today –
I had good leftovers from last night's dinner –
and I didn't want to cook them,
So when he asked about my making
an omelet this morning,
I turned the chore over to him.
And much to my surprise
he took the challenge –
he got the eggs out, cracked them
into a little bowl
then he prepared them with
a swig of water and some salt and pepper.
I got out the omelet pan for him,
suggested he melt
some butter in it, and scramble the eggs
with a fork. And it all worked out perfectly.
He even cut up bits of cheese
to go in the mix and put
some salsa on the side.
I wonder what I can get him
to cook next.

A Small Celebration

A great report from Bob's doctor
saying his prostate is normal,
you don't need surgery,
left us ecstatic and
called for a special celebration.
We opted to have
lunch at a favorite place,
The Ivy, on Robertson Boulevard.
We sat outside like everyone else these days,
a white umbrella protecting us from the sun.
Though we sat closer to the street.
our table, laid formally with
a white starched and ironed tablecloth,
had a flower printed pitcher full of
The Ivy's signature roses
in pinks, purples, reds and yellows.
We sat across from each other,
Bob smiling as he looked at me,
his bruised hand from all the IVs
leaning on his rosy right cheek.
He wore sunglasses hiding his usual
loving eyes, yet the expression on his mouth said it all.
I wanted a record of this day
to show the world
that he definitely looked
as good as he said he felt.
So I snapped that happy face
for posterity. Still I was wary.
He hadn't touched his burger and fries.

Would he eat any of it,
before topping it off with an ice cream sundae
already in the queue?
On the way home we had another treat.
We drove on the streets with
blooming acacia trees on both sides –
quite a sight of profuse yellows to behold.
Now he's down in the living room
sleeping like a baby on our blue couch.
And no, he didn't eat a bite.
I have the picture to prove it.

Not Out of the Woods

The doctor's bottom line today was,
"he's not out of the woods yet,"
and of course, I could see that.
he's still lying in bed mostly sleeping
mostly nonresponsive.
And today he couldn't remember
our son's name or where he was.
So he's worse. Everyday he's worse.
As I sat there looking at him
I kept thinking, will I ever
get him out of there alive?
I summed it up
to my friend this afternoon.
"I don't know if he's going to make it.

At the Hospital

He lies in his hospital bed
with closed eyes, open mouth
barely moving, barely talking.
His lunch came and I used
the automatic bed raiser
to sit him up.
But he wouldn't take a bite,
either by himself or from me.
Instead he continues sleeping.
I feel so helpless.
I can't get him to talk
and eat and be
a human being again.
But I fail at every step
of the way.
Why do I come here at all?

Setbacks

The hospital scene was
worse than ever today
He lay there the whole time
with eyes closed and mouth open
mostly unresponsive.
I did get one or two smiles
but no words at all.
He had to be
under anesthesia yesterday
to get his nose feeding tube
inserted so he can be force fed.
Maybe that's the reason
for this setback. Even the doctor
was dismayed because
they were talking together
right before he had the procedure.
And with all that going on
he's still fiddling with the tubes.
He tried to pull the nose tube out
and he's still trying
to pull out his catheter.
So they restrained his hands.
When I looked at him today
I practically lost all hope
that I'll ever get my husband back.
This is not the man
I've known and loved
all these fifty plus years.

Important Things

I've left Trump
by the wayside
these last few days.
I've got more important
things to write about.
Like my husband's
physical and mental status
and when, for god's sake,
he'll be able to be
infection free and
hospital free and
allowed to finally
come home. I don't
see that light
at the end of the tunnel yet.
Today he still lay there
though his eyes were open more
and he took some tiny bites
of food. But he's still
controlling the shots.
He pulled his feeding tube
out of his nose
and kept his teeth clenched together
when he didn't want his meds.
The last thing I said to him
tonight was, take care of yourself.
He's the only one who can decide
whether he lives or dies.

2. After Death

Counting the Days

It's day two and I'm
practically all alone
thinking about
how can I go on
without him. Will I learn
to handle all the things
he contributed to our lives?
I read emails and texts
from people sympathizing
and saying they are sorry
and want to help
any way they can.
They express love for him
and complement our long lives
together. If only they knew
really knew the pain in my heart,
in my head, in every shaking
finger such that
my whole body
shivers so that
I don't think I can
bear this pain much longer.

The Floodgates

It's like the floodgates have opened.
He's not here
but his and our friends
have come en masse
at least virtually.
Or they have called,
texted, emailed,
and sent bouquets
of white roses and orchids
and lilies.
I don't want any of that.
I almost cringe
when I see more flowers
on the doorstep
What do I need them for?
I remember after my son died
my first clean up job
was to throw out
the dead flowers.
I couldn't stand the smell.
These new flowers
will end up in the can as well.

Resting Easy

Last night I woke four times –
every couple of hours
after vivid dreams
that disappeared from my mind
as soon as I opened my eyes.
I cannot get a good night's sleep
I cannot rest easily
I cannot warm up enough
to stop shaking.
What I need is someone
to hold me while I sleep
so I feel safe and free from the chill
of my life.
And I don't think
that holding warmth
will come any time soon

How Are You Doing?

We're planning Bob's memorial
even though the reality
of his death still hasn't sunk in.
I keep looking for him
in our house,
touching his things
putting his clothes
that were returned
from the hospital
into the hamper
to be washed and ready for him.
People keep asking me how I am doing.
How can I be doing?
After my husband of fifty years died
"I'm not doing" is my answer
though I manage a good pretense.
But people have been so kind and loving.
I'm sure they'll be telling me
of their love
at the memorial.

Missing Tears

I'm not a good crier.
Even during my husband's
memorial service
I hardly shed a tear.
Mostly I sat there
in a daze, shaking such
that I thought
my whole body would break.
He is gone now
just a few hours
short of one week,
and it still is like
a bad horrible awful nightmare.
I cannot conceive
of a happy life without him.
How could our life together
for over fifty years
allow that to happen?

Small Conversations

I find myself
talking about “we”
and “our” lately.
I can’t let go
of him even
in small conversations.
He’s always with me.
It’s not that I care
about that.
It’s not that
I ever want him
out of my life.
It’s just that
I cannot move on
without him
if I continually think
of him as the other
part of me.
Well it’s no wonder.
We were together
for over fifty years
How does one sever
a relationship like that?
How does one dump
the man who was
the love of my life?

Heavy Heart

I first woke
at my usual time
around five o'clock.
But this morning
was different.
I felt a heaviness
in my chest
like my heart was
breaking in two.
And I couldn't get over
that feeling until
I later went
for my big long walk.
This heavy fear
makes sense.
Today photographers
came to take
marketing shots of my house
that will go up for sale
two days from now.
Just the thought
of selling the house
I've lived in
over forty-two years
and the moving away
is more than
my heart can bear
right now.

Abandonment

I feel abandoned
put upon
left to do
all the work.
Arrange for repairs
take care of the garden
sign the listing papers
and make sure
everything is perfect
before a buyer
comes by.
Then I'm the one
left to decide
on an offer
if one ever comes through.
Next I must take care of
all the work
of the move:
the throwing away,
the giving away,
the taking away,
handling all the things
we lovingly bought together
and put into this home.
And touching each
one by one while deciding
what to do with it.
I resent it
I want him by my side.

Finally Sold

We've opened escrow
on the sale of my house.
I electronically signed
the paperwork to
get things going
and now it will
take two months
to make this sale
a reality. I like that
I sold it to
two young doctors
who will raise
their two-year old Auggie
in this house. It has practice
raising little boys
and being a good place
for them to thrive
and grow and love.
I wish this family well.
I wish them years
of happiness here,
in good, warm hands.

Broken

Since my husband died
I've been broken.
I know I give the impression
that I have it all together,
but that is just a white lie
I even tell myself.
I pretend I am strong
I pretend I am getting on
without him. Yet,
I feel how empty life is
now that he is gone.
People tell me
what a loving and caring man
he was and how lucky
I was to have him.
That's why I'm moving,
That's why I've taken on
this change so soon
since he died.
I need to take
the daily reminders
the familiar routines away,
and begin to build new memories
somewhere else.
Maybe then I can repair
the brokenness
and the loneliness
I'm feeling now.

An Anniversary Missed

Today would have been
our fifty-first anniversary.
But today there is nothing
to celebrate. He's been gone
over six months.
How can I celebrate that?
Instead I'm making believe
this is a regular day.
I went to check out
floor coverings at my new apartment
and had a lovely chatty
lunch with my designer,
just as if nothing
is untoward. Only my sister's
caring call brought
me back to reality
and into the realm
of un-forgetfulness.
Yes, Bob, you are truly
with me today
like you are every
other day of the year.

3. The Pandemic

Effects of the Coronavirus

Today the stock market crashed a ton.
I've never seen the DOW go down
over one thousand points
in one day before.
And they say it's because
of the spread of the Coronavirus
that started in China and is now
in South Korea and in Europe.
Where does that leave us?
Did we lose a lot of money today?
Can we still travel anywhere
and stay safe from infection
or should we soon wipe
the supermarket shelves clean
like they've done in Italy?
There's one good result of all this.
Mr. former president can no longer say
he created the best economy in the world.
All the highs of this past year
have been wiped out.

Why I'm Not Afraid

The Coronavirus has surrounded us.
It's cropped up all over the world.
They've declared an emergency
in Los Angeles, and my beloved Italy
has been hit hard.
Yet for some reason, I'm not afraid
even though they say
most older people who get it
will probably die. But I'm
a young older person, always fit
and healthy. Plus I'm washing
my hands and trying my hardest
to keep my hands off my face.
First of all, where would I catch the virus?
And second, if did, I'd get over it fast.
The person I worried over
was my husband Bob,
not me.

The Coronavirus Is Driving Me Nuts

My world has gone nuts.
We're practicing social spacing
or if you prefer,
social distancing. We're coughing
into our tissues, we're washing our hands
every time we turn around,
we're wiping down everything we touch
with sanitary wipes
and we're hoarding, piling things
we don't think we can live without
into our shopping carts
after waiting hours in line
just to get into our favorite discount store.
And what we're hoarding the most
is toilet paper - even though
an average person uses less than
half a roll a week.
I have thirty-six rolls on hand –
a dozen more than my usual stash.
I think that will get me by
for a good part of a year.
Nuts, I say. People are going nuts.

Why Wear a Mask

To wear a mask or not wear a mask
is the question these days.
After all masks are not for protecting us,
they protect those we come
in contact with from our germs.
I was only wearing one in grocery stores
up until a few days ago,
But now I wear one when I walk
especially since our beach promenade
has been opened.
There the crowds are thick
almost back to normal
with walkers, runners, little ones
in baby carriages.
Some wear masks and some do not.
Some practice social distancing
And some do not.
I'm of the belief that if I wear one
to protect them in return
they ought to wear one
to protect me.
How safe we would be
if we all thought that way.
Really how hard is that?

Staying Home

I'm supposed to stay home,
shelter in place,
so to speak until this
Coronavirus is under control
and no more people
are diagnosed and dropping dead.
So why when I went
to take a shower
I picked out good-looking clothes,
definitely unnecessary
While here at home.
Sure, I may go to the store
later today, but I don't need
good attractive clothes
at the grocery store.
So why, I ask myself.
Maybe taking a little bit
of care feels better
than looking like
a real schlump
day after day.
And I even looked in the mirror
to check myself out
after I got dressed.

Maneuvering to Stay Safe

I take a risk every day
during the Coronavirus
shelter at home lockdown.
I have to. If I didn't
go for my daily morning walk
there would be no sense
living at all. Of course,
I try to protect myself,
working diligently to keep six feet away
from people on the path
or street that I'm on.
I also go early enough
to avoid the hordes,
and I stick to places less traveled
than most. But still
others come and go
by me all the time.
Then I must maneuver
around them like a little soft shoe.
I walk to the other side of the street,
I stop in a driveway to let them pass,
or even go so far as walk
in another direction.
Anything to keep away from
on-coming people.
But sometimes I get a surprise –
like this morning when a woman
rounding a corner almost
walked right into me

and a young jogger came up from behind
practically side-swiping my arm.
During those encounters
I get the feeling all could be lost.
I'm doomed, and it's my fault
for being out there at all.
Yet, I still go day after day.
I must. It's my obsessive habit
and well worth the risk.

4. Political Thoughts

Political Campaigns

I can't stand the Democratic presidential campaign.
Each candidate is so mean
to one another.
They interrupt, they speak
over their time limit,
they throw terrible remarks at each other
and they don't even listen. Instead
as soon as one starts to speak
when called on by the moderator,
they raise their arms as high as
they can to call attention
to what they have to say.
It's an embarrassment
that we in the United States
are running a campaign this way.
Before Trump it never used
to be like this.
Now there I go, blaming him again.
Why not? He's created
that mean climate
in our country when
he became our president.
And now it's spilled
over to both parties.

Importance of Voting

I voted today.
I worked on my sample ballot
this morning and filled in
all the bullets
then transferred the data
to my official ballot.
I placed it in the envelope
signed and dated it
and wrote in my address.
Afterward I went to one of
the two official ballot drop off
boxes in Manhattan Beach
and slipped it in.
Now my goal is to get
Bob up and lucid enough
to sign his envelope
so I can cast his ballot too.
I made that my goal today
at the hospital.
The nurse and doctor there
have committed to
make that happen too.

Gone with the Wind

One of the most crushing results
of the George Floyd death
and all the changes we'll
be making to our country
relative to Black Lives Matter
is the treatment of my all-time
favorite book and movie
Gone with the Wind. Of course
I think it's right to take it
off the shelves now.
It was a disgrace the way
black people were portrayed
and how it glorified the Confederacy.
But the beauty of the mansions,
costumes, the romantic lovers,
even the huge fires burning
the city of Atlanta to death,
caught my fancy when I was eleven
and never let go.
Even though I still own
the book and movie,
I will never read or see the movie again.
It's time to treat black lives
like they matter, not
as unpaid, disrespected servants.
I was such a dummy at the time
not to understand what I was
so in love with as a girl.

Political Bomb

It was a bomb.
Yup, his first rally
in three months failed
and failed badly.
Only sixty-two hundred people
took their seats
in the nineteen thousand capacity auditorium
and no people filled
the outside overflow arena.
And of course he blamed
everyone but himself.
The fake news, the protesters,
people on social media who signed up
but never intended to show.
Maybe he's the one
who needs to get his act together
and start governing instead of rallying
and start paying attention
to black lives and Coronavirus victims
instead of only caring about
how many people fill his auditoriums
and getting reelected.
As of now, he certainly doesn't
have that in the bag.

Fearing Forty-five

There's a growing fear
that our never-admit-defeat president
will not concede
or move out of the White House
if he loses the presidential election in November.
He'll find people to blame, fraudulent balloting,
and any other conspiracy theory excuses
for why he didn't lose.
Mr. Biden,
the very likely winner,
has promised to bring in the militia
to take Mr. Trump and his family
out of the White House
with bodily force – though I think
Melania will be glad to go as far away
from him as she can.
The main problem: if he doesn't concede
it could turn into a nightmare
for Mr. Biden. He'll always
have to be looking over his shoulder.

Capitol Tragedy

Huge crowds took over
our United States Capitol building,
barging through the front doors,
infiltrating the chambers
where Congress conducts its business
trespassing Senators offices and rummaging
through their desk drawers.
One woman was shot
and after hours of this siege
they are still all over
the grounds and building.
Why might you ask?
It was ordered by
the president of the United States.
And instead of coming out
to get them to disburse
and let Congress get on
with their business of the day
counting and ratifying
the electoral college votes,
he said to the rioters:
I love you; you are my heroes….
Is there anybody who will take him
bodily out of his White House office
and arrest him
for inciting a riot?

Forty-five Is Gone

It's over!
Forty-fifth's time
in the White House is over.
He left this morning,
flew to his Florida house
at 9 am, and hopefully
will never darken
the White House door again.
We've inaugurated
a real president today,
one with a heart and soul
and years of government
management experience.
After today I'm confident
Joe Biden will unify our current
badly divided American population
and help us all work together
once again.

A Poem for Uvalde, Texas

President Biden
said losing a child
is like tearing
a piece out of your soul.
I know. I lost a son.
And recently nineteen
sets of parents
in Uvalde, Texas
lost their precious
little boys and girls too.
No amount of prayers
will ever take away
their pain.
I know. My pain
stays in my heart
after twenty-three years.
And that we allowed it
to happen.
That we didn't restrict
an eighteen-year-old
from buying
an assault weapon,
designed and intended
only to be used
in battlefields
and not to bloody
schools or grocery stores
or places of worship.
We must stop

these horrors –
the killing of
innocent people
just wanting
to live normal lives.
We must stop
the pain and
the pieces of our souls
from tearing away.

NOW

5. Moving

Giving It All Away

Yesterday my son and daughter-in-law
came over and within two-hour's time
they sorted, checked the pockets
and packed up all of Bob's
slacks, jackets, shirts, ties, sweaters,
shoes, socks into twelve large plastic
garbage bags. I mostly watched
but the whole process
made me exhausted.
I kept asking myself was
I getting rid of his stuff
much too soon. I certainly don't
need the leftover closet space.
Yet there is way more to go.
His papers, books, coins, keepsakes,
must be given away or sold.
Then comes my things.
In at least four to six months
I'll be selling this house
and I have no idea
what is going to become
of all the stuff in it.

Every Day Is the Same

More and more I think
I can't live like this anymore.
There is no place to go
no place to turn to
no one to sit down with
and just talk.
Losing my husband
during the Pandemic
has made mourning him
and finding a way
to get over his death
much, much harder.
It has taken all I have
just to live through each day
to put one foot
in front of the other
and walk, eat, read,
write, watch television
and then go to bed.
The worse part
is that every day
is the same. Every day
I stay here feeling cold
I stay here and feel shaky,
I stay here and feel blue
All alone.

But Why?

I feel like I live
in a fantasy world.
If I get up at a certain time
I can be back from my walk
to do my day. But why?
I don't have much to do
I don't have anyone to talk to
I don't have a reason
to get up early
or dress in a certain way
or shower or wash my hair
or put on my huge supply
of moisturizers. I don't need
any of that anymore.
The only thing I need
is Bob by my side, holding me
snuggling me in our bed
and keeping me warm.

Sleeping Late

I've taken to laze in bed
later and later each day.
I don't want to get up
and face all the nothings
on my daily plate.
Yet after a half hour of so
I uncover, sit up, and swing
my feet around so
I can slide off the bed.
I like to get my walk in.
I still fantasize that
there's someone awaiting me
when I get home.
But of course there's no one.
No one needing me
to make his breakfast.
Just today as I was buying yogurt
I almost bought what I usually bought
for him instead of my
dairy free kind.
I had to remind myself
I don't have to buy for him anymore.

Liquidation Plan

I've been making
a plan for liquidation.
That is, getting rid
of my piles and piles
of things
before I leave this house.
They are on the wall,
in the cabinets,
on the shelves, in the drawers
and every last piece
that I sell, giveaway or throw out
will take a piece out of me.
First in the plan
is to get my sister here
and ask her to take
the silver, jewelry, and object d'art
I inherited from my mother.
I've had them long enough.
Now it's time for them
to live with her.
The other things
I'll offer to my nieces
and nephews. I know
my nephew Mark
wants the big wooden
cutting board with the
silver cow's horn handles.

Filling the Void

Even when I add
a chore or two
to shake up my day
it still ends
the same way.
Eating dinner in front
of the television
I watch a movie.
I watch one each night.
Some good, some bad
but it's a diversion
which I need more
and more of these days.
I don't know how
to get out of this rut,
and when I study it
real closely, I don't think
I ever will.
My husband is gone
and the void he left
in my life will never
go away. And nowadays
I want to yell and scream
at him for leaving me.
Even though he couldn't help
getting so sick,
he needed to get well
and not leave me this way.

Alone Forever

Yes, it's true
I don't think I'll ever
have someone else
to live with and love again.
All the signs are there.
I'm over eighty
I'm losing my looks
I'm very set in my ways
and I can't hear very well.
How could I attract
anyone being like this.
And why should I?
They'd probably want
to be with me for my money
or for me to take care of them.
I don't need people like that.

Getting Ready

My maintenance guy, Freddie,
is helping me get
my house ready for sale.
Yesterday and today
he cleaned out my garage
and painted the walls
and floor with such skill
I could see people wanting
to move right in there
and leaving their cars outside.
He's a short guy but built
like a wrestler. He also has
a bushy beard and head of black hair
with some white strands
running through it.
What's more he's so nice
that I would like to give him a hug
if only COVID would allow it.
This guy knows what he's doing.
Wish I had had him do this work
years ago so I could
have enjoyed it too.

6. Playa Vista

Moving to Playa Vista

Yes, I've decided to move
to Playa Vista and live
in a senior retirement community.
It's a beautiful space
with plenty of room
and lots of light, closets,
and nice bathrooms and kitchen.
Actually more than I need.
Actually more than I want.
All it takes is money
and my willingness to play
with the other people
who live in the other
one hundred seventy-four units.
That makes me worry.
I've been alone for so long –
it's already over six months
since Bob left me.
How will I know how to interact
with others anymore?
Well, living there
will probably force me to.

A Nice New Apartment

I went to visit
my new apartment.
It's still waiting for me.
It looks nice, though
nothing I'm jumping
for joy about.
But these days
I don't get excited
about much of anything.
The place is small.
It has little closet space
though the kitchen
has lots of cabinet room.
But then I look at
my kitchen and closets here.
I know, I'll never fit
all my stuff I'm moving
into the puny space
I'll have there.
So I'll just throw
those damn things out.
I couldn't care less.

Nothing Left

The only part of this move
that bothers me
is having to do the
sorting and packing
and giving it all away.
It is like going through books
page by page,
piece by piece.
It's like I'm
going through my life –
and when I dump the stuff
into a garbage bin
or Goodwill bag
I am doing away
with my life
and all the memories
associated with each item
until there is nothing left.

Community Living

I have to prepare
for a dinner date
with two ladies
tonight.
In fact I have invites
for two more
dinners this week
and one more for next.
Those will be a true test
of my patience
for this kind
of community living.
I chose it and
now I'm not so sure
I made the right decision.
Time will tell
how I'll take to it.
But no matter
how it turns out
I will never move again
except feet first.

Trying Harder

Okay, I'll try
I told my sister.
I'll try to
participate more,
call back the people
who reached out to me.
I know I'm friendly
when I see
someone I know
outside or in the hall,
but nothing seems
to have resulted
from that.
Yet, today I got
a great invite
to join two women
at next week's
Wine Wednesday event.
It's just up my alley.
Those are the kind
of people I want to meet –
not the little old ladies
who drink water
with ice and lemon
to accompany and augment
their dinners. Nah!

For As Long as I Need It

In my eyes
my place is clean.
The furniture placed well
the accessories where they belong.
Of course it doesn't come close
to the home I left –
just over two weeks ago.
I'll never be able
to emulate that.
Now my apartment
will have to do.
Now my new place
will give me shelter
and peace and
a life I can stand
for however long
I need it.

Every Night Is Like Clockwork

It's like clockwork.
I turn on the television
at six o'clock
and don't turn it off
until ten.
I watch news – usually
the Rachel Maddow show,
some Food TV. I especially like
Chopped and Beating Bobby Flay,
And then I take the
little Apple clicker and
find a movie to see
on Netflix or Prime.
Lately I've been watching crap.
Stupid love stories with
young actors I've never heard of.
Last night was an exception.
Diane Keaton played a widow
in Hampstead. An unlikely romance
happens where no one
would have expected it.
After television I write
a daily journal entry.
Then I'm off to bed
to read my latest book
for a few minutes.

It's Not Too Bad

The last moving boxes
are empty.
Seven weeks later
I've finally finished
the awful chore
of packing, unpacking,
putting away, and
giving and throwing away.
And I must say
the stuff in
my new apartment
doesn't look too bad.
Sure the shelves
are a little crowded
with things I
couldn't part with,
but what the hell.
I look at
the Waterford crystal
bright and shining
in my China closet
And think,
Ben will have
a great time
getting rid of
all that someday.

I've Unlocked My Door

I went home this morning.
I drove to Manhattan Beach
parked by the library
and took my ever familiar
walk to the beach and
on the Strand. I could have
stayed for hours, this day
is so beautiful. But
twelve thousand steps
was my limit.
Then I ate my favorite breakfast
at my favorite breakfast place –
avocado toast at
Le Pain Quotidien. That really
made my day and made me
happier than I've been
for weeks. I'm going
to do that again
and again, and again.
There is nothing to keep
me locked up here.

Missing My Strawberry Marina

I walk by a patch
of strawberry marina trees
every morning.
They have red trunks,
dark green leaves
and tiny bunches
of berries hanging
from their branches.
I had a strawberry marina
planted in my garden
on Valley Drive.
It gave me great pleasure.
So these on Westlawn
bring back fond
memories of home.
But sometimes
those memories
make me so, so sad,
that I don't live
on Valley Drive anymore.

Keeping Busy

The end of a sad week
as the days start
to get cooler and clearer
and busier. I like
the busy part.
I'm socializing more
and feeling better
about myself and
where I live. It's like
I have to force myself
to get up and get out
or else I would
sleep all day long.
People say they are
happier and more comfortable
in their own apartments.
Like they have agoraphobia
or the Stockholm syndrome
that started with COVID.
Well, I've decided not
to succumb. I feel much better
taking a walk with a friend
then curled up like a ball
on my couch sleeping it off.

7. Daily Life

Learning from the News

I've been listening to podcasts lately
learning all kinds of things
I never thought important to learn.
Today I heard from a man
who wrote a book called *When,*
like in what times during the day
are best for us to have a surgery,
take a nap, start school, wake.
It all depends on whether
we're a morning person or someone
who stays up late and gets up late.
He says young children love the mornings
while teenagers don't even wake their bodies
until noon. So it makes sense
that some schools have changed
their start time to nine am.
I've always been a morning person.
While listening I was halfway through
my ninety-minute walk at eight am.
No wonder I crash in the afternoon.
He also has thoughts on how long
our naps should be. Well, for sure
I over exceed on that.

Rationalizations

I wouldn't exactly
call it writer's block.
I can find plenty
of things to write
in poetry, in prose,
in journal entries.
But writing for
my memoir class
has put a bit
of pressure on me.
Everyone there writes
with such skill
about subjects
so personal and timely
that I have resorted
to going back
in my files
to pull up old pieces
rather than start anew.
I rationalize,
I excuse myself,
thinking they don't
know me.
They haven' heard
any of this before
so how bad could
it be if I read about
my ex-husband, someone
they probably didn't
even know I had.

Clashing Colors

For probably the second time
I'm sitting in the residence living room.
It is large, lavishly furnished
and has a carpet that brings to mind
sprays of Matisse's flowers
on a clear blue lake.
But I don't like it.
The colors clash with the couches
and chairs in shades
of orange and turquoise
with an occasional beige thrown in.
Whomever designed this room
must have wanted to shock
and definitely succeeded disturbing
my senses. But I'm happy to say,
I don't have to live here.
It's the people's living room.
No wonder it's always empty.

Please Believe Me

I keep saying
I don't need anything.
And up until yesterday
I've refrained from
buying anything.
But today
I bought a puffer jacket
and puffer vest.
Plus I bought them
at a huge discount.
Then I went
to Ralph's for more wine
and a few food items.
Later I shopped on Amazon
for the things on
my Ralph's list I couldn't find:
Cedar wood moth repellant
and clothes hangers.
I never could stand
wire hangers in my closet.
Hopefully my bank account
will forgive me when I say.
I'll never do it again.
I wonder if it will believe me.

Raining in California?

Rain has come
to Southern California.
Much needed but
for me a huge annoyance
at first since it interfered
with my morning walk.
However, I found a substitute.
I went to the gym in my building
and walked for an hour and
twenty minutes on the treadmill
and racked up over ten
thousand steps.
The tread-walk was faster
than my outside walks.
So what is so
bad about that?
Let it rain, let it pour.
I don't mind a bit.

Unlucky Thursday

I used to say Thursday
was my unlucky day.
Something must have happened
during high school or
my first marriage to make
me think that way.
But after we found
Paul dead in the bathtub
on a Thursday morning,
I knew for sure,
I needed to stay in bed
with the covers over my head
so I wouldn't have
to experience another
Thursday like that.
Now it doesn't really matter.
I moved here on a Wednesday,
Bob died on a Sunday.
Now I feel
all days are unlucky
whether it's a Thursday or not.
I don't like any of them.

My Famous Painting

It is not a famous painting
except in my mind.
It's by my dear friend
since 1961. She is a recognized
artist with hangings in
the Smithsonian and
the Clinton Whitehouse.
She painted Bob and me
in a beautiful embrace –
our arms around each other
our smiles and our eyes
shining with love.
Bob wears his favorite
brightly colored silk shirt,
I wear a plain tee accessorized
with pearls. That painting
completed in 1998, hung
in the dining room of our house,
Now it's in the entry hall
of my new apartment.
It's so large it takes up
an entire wall.
That's good. I want
everyone to see it
and know what
a loving, caring, good man
my husband was.

Breaking the Rules

I think we broke the rules last night.
We went out for dinner
but only to a friend's house.
She cooked and it was wonderful.
Not just to eat delicious food
with them, but to have a conversation
with folks other than ourselves.
We've decided this is a good way
to interact with others –
small dinners at home, since we can't eat
out in restaurants
or sit at bars or go to the movie theaters.
All the things we rely on for diversions
have been relegated to what
we can find to do at home.
Luckily, we have music and streamed movies
right into our television screens
and our ear buds. Plus, we can always
snuggle in with a good book.
My shelves are bursting with books unread
just crying for some much-needed attention
right now.

Spending Time

As I walked today
surrounded by
nothing but beauty
and warmth
I considered how
I will spend my time.
I can just sit
at my computer
and write my day away,
I can finish updating all
my credit and debit accounts,
I can go shopping
for new baby gifts,
I can read Sontag's
novel, *In America*,
which is finally
gaining my interest,
or I can continue
following the Putin
aggression in Ukraine,
which has taken my time
ad infinitum since it started.
Or like I'm thinking
right now – do
all of the above.
Another thought,
go back outside where
it's still beautiful.

The Dating Game

I started setting up
a Match.com account
though I stopped short
of posting my picture.
I have mixed feelings
about online dating,
actually about any
dating at all.
My friend has gone
on a couple dates
with men she's met
on Match, and
not surprisingly,
they were duds.
Ugly, fat, though smart,
these men were not her type –
and not attractive enough.
As I scrolled through
the group of pictures
and data about the men
offered, I thought,
they were duds too.

My Little Niece

The adorable
two-year old
with the long
flowing red hair
has taken my
heart. Her giggle
and smile, her
I can do it mood,
her willingness
to eat everything
and try foods
she's never had before.
Plus she pats
her baby brother hello,
and doesn't see him
as a threat.
She asked me
to pick her up,
And very willingly
I gathered her
in my arms –
all thirty pounds of her.

Compost Collection

I just came back
from dumping
vegetable waste
into the compost heap
at the Farmer's Market.
It's a short ten-minute
walk from where I live
though I wish
our management
would provide
a compost receptable here.
Our environment needs
help anyway it can get it.
Each day I save my
veggie leftovers
in a big baggie
and keep it in the freezer
so it won't smell.
And most Saturdays
I walk it away.
We need to conserve
water as well.
California is experiencing
a huge drought as I write.
Now don't get me started
on red meat!

Why I Write

I say I write
a poem a day.
But is my writing
really poetry
or just a way
to place my words
on the page?
I write about
the goings on
in my life,
my cares, worries,
and sometimes
a joy or two.
But mostly these
few words are
meaningless, and
best left unwritten
and off the page.

Maybe Tomorrow

Like magic the wet skies turned blue
the cool air turned warm and I
started to relish my morning walks
again. And it seems so have the others.
They are now out in force with smiles
on their faces as they pass me by –
some pushing carriages, some reigning
in the pups on long leashes, some
running at high speeds, some moving
around the traffic on limitless bikes.
I just go at my usual pace – a pretty
good clip for an eighty-plus year old
woman, never letting up, until I reach
my goal. I do the same route every
day unless I give myself a treat and
walk the Manhattan Beach Strand.
That's where I want to be – always!
Or maybe tomorrow!

www.ingramcontent.com/pod-product-compliance
Lightning Source LLC
Chambersburg PA
CBHW022201160726
48282CB00024B/282
9788119228393